THE
NORTH NORFOLK
RAILWAY

•A PAST and PRESENT COMPANION•

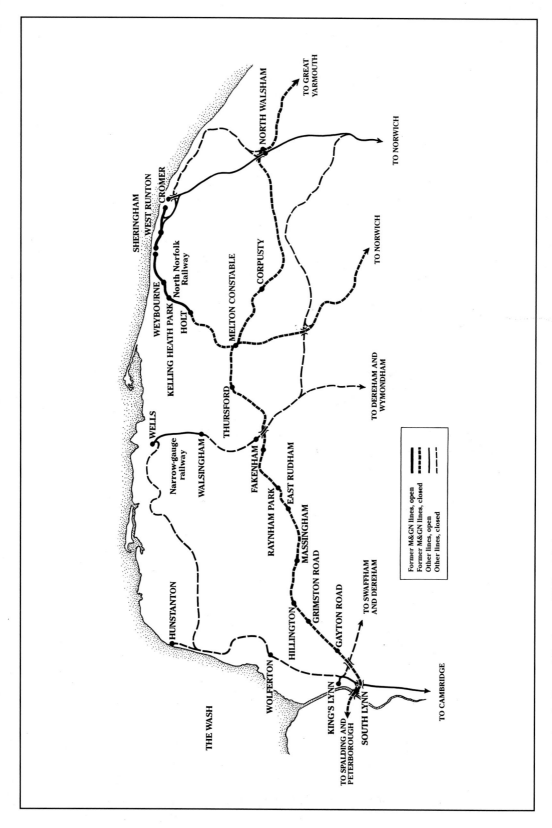

Map showing the lines of the former Midland & Great Northern Joint Railway and connecting lines in Norfolk, including the North Norfolk Railway.

THE
NORTH NORFOLK RAILWAY

· A PAST and PRESENT COMPANION ·

*A nostalgic trip along the whole route
from South Lynn to Cromer*

Adrian Vaughan

· RAILWAY HERITAGE ·
from
The NOSTALGIA *Collection*

For Phyllis and Raymond for years of kindness

First published in August 1998
Reprinted September 1999

British Library Cataloguing in Publication Data

A catalogue record for this book is available from the British Library.

ISBN 1 85895 130 5

Past & Present Publishing Ltd
The Trundle
Ringstead Road
Great Addington
Kettering
Northants
NN14 4BW

Tel/Fax: 01536 330588
email: sales@slinkp-p.demon.co.uk

Map drawn by Christina Siviter

Printed and bound in Great Britain

| Past and Present |

A Past & Present book
from
The NOSTALGIA Collection

ACKNOWLEDGEMENTS

I am indebted to Brian Fisher for his warm-hearted generosity in giving me a free run of his large photographic collection of the North Norfolk Railway. I am equally indebted to Geoff Gowing of the Midland & Great Northern Joint Railway Society for waiving reproduction fees, and for the same reason to Mr David Whitehead of the Photographic Department of Eastern Daily Press. The great goodwill generated everywhere for the North Norfolk Railway is very heartening. I must also thank Raymond Meek, for applying his great knowledge of the M&GN to my text, and to Phyllis Youngman, for her good humour and refreshments during my consultations with Raymond. I must thank Frank Shuttleworth, custodian of the M&GN Society's photograph archive and his wife Carol for her kindness; Fred Poynter, for the use of his library and for his practical knowledge of the railway; and David Madden, General Secretary and General Manager of the North Norfolk Railway from 1965 to 1995, who helped with the history and kindly found two colour transparencies with the rarity of hens' teeth.

Thanks too to Member No 9, Bernard Amies; to Ian Hurst, whose generosity helped save the Kelling Extension for posterity; to Keith Montague, Chairman of the Company; and to John Tinkler, General Manager, for their kind assistance.

Last but not least, thanks to 'Fozzy' and Allan Colley for their help in making certain pictures possible.

CONTENTS

Railway recreated: an evocative photograph taken by the author from the down platform at Weybourne station, looking towards Holt, at around 8 pm on 30 August 1997 after a long day as signalman in Weybourne signal box. *AV*

Sheringham station looking west in 1960, and transformed as the headquarters of the North Norfolk Railway in April 1998. *Stations UK (R20720)/AV*

INTRODUCTION

The North Norfolk Railway (NNR), from Sheringham to Holt, is a 5½-mile fragment surviving from a lost system of railways amounting to about 183 route miles that once connected the Midland Railway and the Great Northern Railway with the City of Norwich, Cromer, Yarmouth, and, by an associated line, Lowestoft. The North Norfolk Railway is not quite the last surviving fragment of this hydra-headed system, for the section from Cromer to Sheringham was also a part of it, and the two pieces of railway, though in very different forms of ownership, look at each other at Sheringham over a gap of a mere 150 yards and the dream is of reunion.

The story of what is now the North Norfolk Railway began with the Lynn & Fakenham Railway (L&FR), promoted by a speculative railway building company, Wilkinson & Jarvis of London. This firm obtained its authorising Act of Parliament on 13 July 1876, the Act empowering the company to compulsorily purchase land, to raise capital and to build a single-track railway from 'Gaywood Junction' – forking east from the Hunstanton line of the Great Eastern Railway (GER) on the outskirts of King's Lynn, to a junction with the GER at Fakenham. Wilkinson & Jarvis were the engineers and builders of their lines, and also raised all the money for legal and engineering purposes, so they constructed the lines as cheaply as possible in order to make the most profit when they came to sell them. They hoped that the GER would buy their line to prevent it from falling into the hands of the Great Northern or Midland companies who had been probing towards Norfolk for many years.

The L&FR was opened in stages over the 21 miles and reached Fakenham on 16 August 1880 – but its terminus was not at the GER station on the east of the town, but at a separate station a mile away on the west side, in the parish of Hempton. Between getting their Act and opening their line, Wilkinson & Jarvis may have become aware of the GER's reluctance to purchase, and instead came to an arrangement with Sir Edmund Lacon who had financed a railway from Yarmouth to North Walsham in a westerly drive to break out of the GER monopoly of his home town of Yarmouth. This route arrived in North Walsham in 1881.

On 12 August 1880, Wilkinson & Jarvis obtained an Act authorising them to construct a railway from Fakenham to Melton Constable, and from there to construct a branch line to Holt and the rapidly silting port of Blakeney, and onwards from Melton to Norwich. Blakeney had been the target of several railway schemes over the years, none of them getting beyond a mere proposal, and this one was no different. On 11 August 1881 the L&FR abandoned Blakeney when it obtained an Act to build a railway from Kelling – on the line of the proposed and now abandoned Blakeney scheme – 4½ miles to Sheringham, where the station was to be sited '370 yards south-west of the fountain', and from there another 3⅜ miles to Cromer, 'near the cemetery'. The proposed Kelling-Blakeney line was to have diverged from the actual Kelling-Cromer line, as built, immediately on the east side of the existing Bridge 299. The L&FR purchased an extra width of land to the west of this bridge, and it is this extra land that is now used as the site of the NNR's Holt station. On 18 August 1882 the L&FR amalgamated with Sir Edmund Lacon's railway from Yarmouth to North Walsham and the small companies connecting Lynn with Spalding, Bourne and Peterborough, to form the Eastern & Midlands Railway (E&MR).

The Holt, Norwich and North Walsham lines were built under the supervision of a young man – William Marriot – only just out of his apprenticeship as an engineer with the famous Ipswich firm of Ransome & Rapier. In 1881 he was on the point of emigrating to the USA when he was recruited by Mr Jarvis as assistant to his man in the area, Byers, and after only six weeks

Marriot was appointed Resident Engineer in Norfolk for Wilkinson & Jarvis. Marriot was young and full of a wonderful, boyish enthusiasm for his work. According to him everyone concerned with the construction of the L&FR and later E&MR lines were jolly fine fellows, good-naturedly working hard, playing cards and sportingly whacking each other with the flats of their spades or indulging in manly fisticuffs when disputes arose. Once, during a game of cards, a player died, but the game had to be finished so they propped the corpse up in a corner until it was completed (*40 Years of a Norfolk Railway,* William Marriot, M&GN Publications).

The line from Fakenham to Norwich was opened on 2 December 1882, and that from Melton to North Walsham on 5 April 1883. There was now an unbroken route from York, London King's Cross and the Midlands to Norwich and Yarmouth, although it involved a reversal of the train at King's Lynn, and also at Peterborough for trains coming from the Midland Railway.

The Secretary of the E&MR, E. B. Reid, told the Board of Trade that the Melton-Holt line would be ready for inspection on 28 September. Major-General Hutchinson came on the 29th by special train to Melton Constable where he was treated to a very judicious luncheon in Marriot's office before he set out to inspect the 6½ miles to Holt. He found the line to be safe and gave at once his permission for it to be opened for passenger traffic. In the report he made on 3 October he said: 'The steepest gradient is 1 in 80 [never say Norfolk is flat] and there is a 14-chain curve into Melton. There are some high embankments and deep cuttings. The bridges are of concrete, faced with brick, and there is a footbridge entirely in timber. The Company have undertaken to work the line by Train Staff & Ticket and until Holt is equipped with a turntable only tank engines may be used subject to a maximum speed of 25 mph.' He might also have mentioned that the single platform at Holt was made of old sleepers and the building thereon was a wooden shed, the original station at Yarmouth (Beach) (*40 Years of a Norfolk Railway*). This building is now at Melton Constable adjoining the present-day Country Club, which in Marriot's day was the M&GN's technical school for apprentices' further education. The Melton-Holt line was opened to passenger traffic without any ceremony with the 6.45am Melton to Holt train on 1 October 1884.

Although the E&MR was an independent company, it had the appearance of a branch line from the GER's Hunstanton line at Gaywood Road Junction, Lynn. If the true east-west-and-London through route was to be realised, Lynn (GER) would have to be bypassed, so a new railway was planned. It was to start from a point 2 miles west of Grimston Road on the existing single line, where there was already a siding serving a sandpit known as 'Bawsey Siding' (its points operated from a ground frame), and it would swing away north-west for Lynn. Meanwhile a double track would continue westwards and bend around to the south-west to circle Lynn and meet the line coming in from Sutton Bridge. To encourage the company in this project, the GNR and the MR gave the E&MR the impression that they would divert their traffic, then passing in and out of Norfolk over the GER, to the E&MR. The very impecunious Wilkinson & Jarvis – and possibly Charles Waring, the contractor of the lines west of Lynn – raised £150,000 by promising investors 5 per cent interest – a rate of return on a 4½-mile railway that would never be earned but which, they hoped, could be paid out of the earnings of the E&MR system as a whole.

A signal box with an 18-lever frame was erected to control Bawsey Junction. It was inspected on 21 October 1885 but found to be sub-standard; the mistakes were rectified, and the box passed as fit on 4 December. The line from this point to the junction with the line coming in from Sutton Bridge was opened on 1 January 1886. At first there was no passenger station at Lynn, but shortly a simple double-track station, called South Lynn, was opened just east of the River Ouse where the Saddlebow Road bridge crossed the line. The line to the GER was retained at South Lynn, but the original L&FR line from Bawsey to the Hunstanton line was abandoned except for a short length at the Bawsey end, used for the sandpits.

The E&MR route from South Lynn eastwards was double track to Grimston Road and single from there to Melton Constable, with crossing places at Hillington, Massingham, Raynham Park, Thursford, Melton, Holt, Sheringham and Cromer; East Rudham station was converted to a crossing place in October 1886.

The Melton-Sheringham line was close to completion when on 26 May 1887 the Board of

Trade received a letter from Lt G. A. Ellis, RN, Inspecting Officer of Coastguards, Wells-next-the-Sea. Ellis may have been an inefficient horseman and was thus perturbed at the approach of the railway. He took little trouble to verify his facts before he wrote, but complained, rather self-importantly, as follows:

'As the Midlands & Eastern [sic] are about to open a line between Holt and Cromer in the County of Norfolk, and as I understand that an Inspector is expected, shortly, to "pass" the line, I venture to bring to your notice that for a considerable distance – not far short of a mile I should think – the rail runs parallel and very close to the High Road between Weybourne and Sheringham and in consequence accident, fatal or otherwise, arising from frightened or runaway horses must only be a matter of time and probably not a long time.

I would venture to suggest respectfully that a system of signalling should be adopted whereby travellers on the High Road would be informed of the approach of a train in time to avoid that part of the road in dangerous proximity to the line whilst a train was in transit over that section of the line. That I have frequently to ride or drive on the above road in the discharge of my office will, I trust, be accepted as sufficient apology for my calling attention to this subject.

I have the honour to be, Sir,

Your obedient servant,

G. A. Ellis'

The Holt-Cromer line was inspected by Major-General Hutchinson for the Board of Trade on 4 June 1887. He reported that it was 11 miles 12 chains long with ten over-line and six under-line bridges made of concrete, faced with brick. There were stations at Sheringham and Cromer. The former had a raised signal cabin with 12 working levers and two spares, while the latter place had 18 and two spare. The interlocking was correct and the line was to be worked with the electric tablet system. Hutchinson bore in mind Ellis's complaint and remarked:

'As regards Lt Ellis's complaint I find that a screen has been erected along that part of the line to which the road most closely approaches, a distance of about 200 yards. In addition to this the Sheringham station Down signals can be seen from the road when driving towards Sheringham and I suggested to Mr Marriot that the Up starting signal post be raised so as to make it visible from the road. This is all that can reasonably be done.'

He also ordered that a level crossing with a gatehouse be established on Kelling Heath because otherwise the railway would bisect the Heath and prevent people from crossing it from east to west. The Holt to Cromer line was duly opened on 16 June 1887.

From 2 July of that year the GNR began to send express trains over the E&MR between King's Cross and Cromer; in the up direction the 8 am Cromer restaurant car express arrived in 'the Cross' at 1.30 pm. By 1889 the GNR had five express trains to Cromer, covering the distance in 4½ hours. The 2 pm King's Cross-York dropped a slip coach at Peterborough for Cromer at 3.25 pm, an average speed to Peterborough of 54 mph. The coach was attached to a fast train from Peterborough to Cromer, but first this had to wait 20 minutes for the arrival (if it was on time) of an express from Manchester so as to provide a holiday connection for passengers from Lancashire, Derbyshire and Nottingham.

The Cromer express than had to traverse 37 miles of single track, calling at Wisbech and Sutton Bridge before South Lynn, arriving there at 4.48. Leaving South Lynn the train climbed over the GER main line on a 1 in 92 gradient and continued to climb thence into the Norfolk heights on sections as steep as 1 in 100, slowing down at each station to collect the staff or tablet for the next stretch of single line. The 47 miles from South Lynn to Cromer were scheduled to take 99 minutes with calls at Fakenham, Melton Constable and Sheringham, arriving at 6.15 having achieved an average speed of 29 mph. But these simple figures do not convey the 'hammer and tongs' glory of what the locomotivemen achieved – for the engines were no stronger than they should have been and their loads were heavier than they ought to have been. Professor Ackworth, chronicler of Victorian railways, in his *Railways of England* published in 1889, wrote, 'What the Eastern & Midlands lacks in capital it makes up for in energy.' The Professor should have been more specific: it was the company that lacked the capital and it was the workers who made up for that with their energy and loyalty. Unfortunately for the loyal and hard-working footplatemen of the E&MR, the GER was able to take its passengers from London to Cromer in 3 hours.

The GNR sent most of its Norfolk traffic over the E&MR, but the wicked Midland used the GER through Peterborough and Thetford. E&MR profits were low and the share price was equally so. This suited the Midland, which was a very expansionist concern, having not so long before purchased the ramshackle Somerset & Dorset Railway. The E&MR wanted higher profits so as to sell itself for a higher price, and went twice to the courts of law to enforce the traffic agreement it thought it had with the Midland, but to no avail. It offered itself for sale to the friendly GNR but was rejected.

Since 1887 the Midland Railway had been planning a route from its Nottingham-London line at Saxby, 4¼ miles east of Melton Mowbray, across the GNR main line at Little Bytham, to Bourne, thus gaining access to Norfolk without the tremendous southwards detour through Stamford and Peterborough. In January 1889 the Midland and the Great Northern companies jointly purchased the routes of the E&MR from Bourne and Peterborough to South Lynn. The Midland even then had a Bill in Parliament for a railway from Saxby to Bourne, which became an Act on 24 June. The E&MR had borrowed far more than it could repay, and in spite of the heroic efforts and low wages of its staff it was heading for bankruptcy. In September 1891 the Midland and the Great Northern offered to purchase the remaining, eastern, section, and the deal was finally sealed on 1 July 1893 when the two main-line companies agreed jointly to pay £1.2 million, which was supposed to guarantee the shareholders 3 per cent interest on their investments. The historian of the GNR, Charles H. Grinling, stated in his definitive history that £1.2 million 'was a decidedly low price, and when the seaside traffic is developed the bargain is likely to prove to have been a very good one for the Great Northern.'

The Midland's Saxby & Bourne Railway opened to goods traffic on 5 June 1893 and to passenger trains on 1 May 1894. Thus came into existence the famous Midland & Great Northern Joint Railway, the product of speculative investment, some sharp practice and a great deal of hard labour on behalf of its men. The latter gave it their all, and its soubriquet 'Muddle & Get Nowhere' was the most undeserved nickname ever inflicted on a railway.

The shareholders of the GNR and Midland voiced their disapproval of the purchase – the investment, they feared, would reduce their dividends – but the Directors of the two companies started to spend large sums to improve their new railway. By 1906 a further £2 million had been spent and a large increase in traffic was expected from developing North Norfolk and its coastal towns. The railway was doubled from Raynham Park eastwards through Melton to Corpusty and from Melton to Briningham on the Holt line. Weybourne station was built and opened in 1901. The effect of these railways in North Norfolk was variable, but at its most dramatic the effect can still be seen at the one-time industrial village of Melton Constable – which was built by the E&MR/M&GN – and Sheringham, which was a very poor fishing hamlet of 400 souls until the M&GN turned it into a seaside resort.

The resident population of Sheringham trebled between 1880 and 1914, and the M&GN lent its cranes for the construction of a sea wall with promenade and also materially assisted in the laying of sewers without which hotels and boarding houses could not be built. The large increase in the number of these establishments, and indeed in ordinary homes, increased the amount of coal and many other necessaries of life, which the railway alone could bring into the district. The Midland and Great Northern companies could offer these tempting seaside destinations to their huge, industrial populations. While the total £3.25 million invested in the M&GN was not welcomed by the shareholders, the money was well spent as regards the improvement it made in the lives of many people in rural Norfolk.

M&GN records show that the increase in originating traffic at Sheringham tended to be for local destinations. In 1896 three season tickets and 31,487 ordinary tickets were sold there for a tiny revenue of £2,166, so the tickets must have been for local destinations. In that same year 1,095 head of cattle were sent away and 3,653 tons of coal brought in. The cost of running the station was put at £339, so it was a much more profitable location than Melton Constable, which had two junctions, two signal boxes and a lot of staff, simply to act as an interchange point without a correspondingly great amount of originating traffic.

Traffic and revenue increased every year up to the end of 1916 – when the government more or less banned holiday traffic. After the war the popularity of Sheringham continued unabated and in 1922 55 season tickets were sold at the station along with 76,087 ordinary tickets for a total passenger income of £15,594. Nearly 3,000 head of cattle were sent away, while 8,523 tons of coal and 4,845 tons of other goods came in. The total cost of running the station was £3,422, owing to a change in the value of money due to wartime and post-war inflation and because men worked an 8-hour day instead of 12 or 15, so more had to be employed.

Today Weybourne seems thoroughly *undeveloped* by the railway, but around 1906 a German called Crundell, or Krundell, built the huge Weybourne Springs Hotel in the woods above the railway to the west of the lane. He also had a siding, bearing his name, to the east of Bridge 299 on Kelling Heath, on the south side of the line, which was intended to carry sand from his pits to the main line. He would have been interned during the Great War, and sold his siding to the M&GN in 1916 when his hotel was commandeered as a military hospital and ambulance trains came regularly to Weybourne. My friend, the late Percy Youngman, whose father was Station Master at Weybourne during the Great War, told me that as a boy of nine or ten years old he saw the ambulance trains arrive – by day or night – and saw the injured soldiers laid on their stretchers, shoulder to shoulder along the platform, the mud of Flanders still on their boots, bloody bandages swathing their heads, limbs or bodies.

After the Great War the erstwhile hotel became a home for mentally handicapped people and in 1941 it was blown up by the Army as it was considered to be too conspicuous a landmark, high on the hill above the village. It was said that if the navigator of a ship aligned the hotel directly behind the tower of Weybourne church he had a perfect line into the deep-water beach where the cliffs fell down to water level. One wonders if this is why a German built a large hotel at remote Weybourne, and one recollects that the Germans had been planning the 1914 war since 1896.

Holt's permanent station, built in red and yellow brick, was opened on 2 November 1886, but this was destroyed by fire in 1926 and a third station was built using concrete bricks made at Melton Works. Holt was little changed by the railway. It is, even to this day, a small town or large village. The lane from Hempstead crossed the line at a skew angle on the level at the east end of the station, and the gates were operated from a signal box containing a gate wheel and 27 levers, of which only 17 were working. To the east of the level crossing, on the south side of the line, a siding led down into a large, deep, quarry-like ballast pit. Although the Holt bypass now occupies the station site and trackbed, the ballast pit, filled with trees, remains.

The Midland & Great Northern Joint, like its sister railway the Somerset & Dorset Joint (Midland and London & South Western), was not included in the Grouping of the companies in 1921 and retained its separate identity until it was absorbed by the London & North Eastern Railway group (LNER) on 1 October 1936; then on 1 January 1948 the erstwhile M&GN was taken into State ownership.

The ex-M&GN system, with the exception of the line from Melton Constable to Cromer, was closed at the end of the day's service on 28 February 1959. Closure brought about the immediate lifting of the track – and also brought into being the Midland & Great Northern Joint Railway Society (MGNJRS). This was at first a small group of furiously outraged lovers of the M&GN. With anti-nationalisation idealism glowing in their breasts as incandescent as coal in a locomotive's firebox, they hoped to buy the line from North Walsham to Yarmouth, 22 miles with 22 level crossing and two bridges over rivers (which short list in itself shows why the M&GN was closed in the age of the motor-car). This exercise succeeded in instilling in the would-be private operators a large dose of realism, and this scheme, together with four subsequent ones, failed to save a piece of the M&GN. In hindsight this was just as well, because it was perhaps the most scenic part of the system that was ultimately saved. The MGNJRS could not, legally, run a railway, so it formed 'Central Norfolk Enterprises' (CNE) as the operating company and continued to raise money in preparation for an eventual purchase of some piece of the line, and did so very aptly by running rail tours over threatened branch lines.

Passenger services continued from Norwich to Melton via Cromer until 4 April 1964 when the section from Melton to Sheringham (exclusive) was closed. Weybourne signal box had been taken out of use on 6 June 1961 and was demolished before October 1963. The demolition of Sheringham West box followed the 1964 closure. In 1965 the MGNJRS, in the guise of CNE, entered into negotiations with British Railways (BR) to purchase the railway land between Weybourne and Sheringham, Sweet Briar Lane, otherwise known as Golf Links Crossing. While these discussions were going on, BR had sold the track from Holt to the Crossing to scrap-metal dealers Kings of Norwich, who at once lifted the track from Kelling Crossing to the east end of the platforms at Weybourne station. This particular length had been flat-bottomed rail and Kings wanted it for re-sale.

Through the generosity of one or two members, CNE purchased Weybourne station and the land from the 40 milepost, 50 yards west of the station, to Golf Links Crossing. From the Crossing into Sheringham the track was still in use by BR. Messrs Kings sold enough of the unlifted track from Kelling Crossing westwards for CNE to relay a railway from milepost 40, through Weybourne station to connect with the existing track going east to Sheringham. The

All the best railways depend on the heavy manual labour of committed workers, as here during the relaying of the Kelling Extension just beyond Springbeck bridge in February 1983. *Brian Fisher (T31/07)*

rails were dragged two at a time behind a farm tractor a minimum of 1½ miles to Weybourne, and the sleepers were loaded into a trailer and driven the 1½ miles over the ballast, which was deeply indented with cavities every 3 feet where the original sleepers had been removed.

Early in 1967 British Railways vacated Sheringham station in favour of a primitive platform, open to the elements, on the east side of the level crossing, and shortly afterwards they demolished the buildings on the old up platform. CNE seems to have had the use of the station without a formal tenancy agreement. Their first instalment of locomotives and rolling-stock came into Sheringham station, over the level crossing, on 4 June 1967. Amongst these were CNE's first motive power – two German-built diesel railbuses, Nos 79960 and 79963, which had worked on Essex branch lines. These proved useful in hauling works trains as well as occasionally performing for private parties before the line was officially opened. Also in that June consignment were two, non-working, steam locomotives, 'J15' 0-6-0 No 564 and 'B12' 4-6-0 No 8572. The first working steam locomotive to arrive on the railway was a Peckett-built 0-6-0 tank, which was delivered by road from Ashington Colliery on 14 April 1969. This engine was informally known as 'Dougal' (because of its supposed resemblance to the dog of that name in the then popular TV series *The Magic Roundabout*), but was later formally named *John D. Hammer* in honour of an NNR volunteer who had died at his workplace attempting to rescue a colleague from a fatal situation. Later arrivals at Sheringham were the 0-4-0 tank engines *Pony*, in 1969, and *Colwyn*, in 1971.

As from 1 July 1969 CNE changed its name to the North Norfolk Railway, and on the same day took up a formal tenancy of Sheringham station and the track out to Golf Course Crossing. The NNR would rent Sheringham station at £1,650 per annum for five years and, subject to review at the end of that time, would continue as tenants for 25 years. This agreement also gave the NNR space to create the present-day No 3 platform road and Nos 4 and 5 sidings. BR also agreed to sell the track running the length of Sheringham's platforms for £2,225 (plus VAT). Finally, the agreement stated that, in principle, BR had no objection to the company acquiring the freehold of Sheringham station at some future date. For several years discussions were carried on between the NNR and BR on this vital point.

In December 1969 the NNR issued £20,000-worth of shares; this was the first time since before the Second World War that a railway company had offered shares to the public. By January 1970 £16,499-worth had been taken up, and with this capital behind them the NNR felt confident enough to offer to buy the track from Golf Links to the end of the line at Sheringham – and to ask British Railways to re-open the line by obtaining a Light Railway Order (LRO). Members of the public could not be carried on trains without an LRO, although the NNR was able to run private trains, for shareholders and 'Members Only', on certain occasions. One of the first of these had been run on 6 August 1969 when the Peckett hauled the Gresley 'quad-art' coaches to Weybourne and back.

In 1969 Sheringham Council wanted to carry out road widening in the vicinity of the level crossing and BR wanted the NNR to pay £2,000 per annum to make good the road/rail surface, which money the company could not pay. Consequently the 150 yards of track between BR and the NNR was lifted on 28 January 1970.

In February 1973 the BR Estate Department offered the Weybourne-Holt trackbed to the NNR, and the latter took over the section on a 'care and maintenance' basis. British Railways, on behalf of the NNR, had to obtain a Light Railway Order, then a further application had to be made to the Ministry to have it transferred to the NNR. The LRO was granted to BR on 14 March 1973, and in that year BR agreed to sell to the NNR for £2,000 the 250 yards of track and land from Golf Links to the Church Street bridge and the bridge itself. BR retained possession of the site east of the bridge while the NNR owned the track on the site.

The next stage was to have the LRO transferred from BR to the NNR and to do this the volunteers had to convince the Ministry of Transport that they were as competent railwaymen and engineers as BR. This entailed bringing the railway, the track, stations and rolling-stock and the competence of the volunteer staff of operators up to a standard approved by BR. The Light Railway (Transfer) Order was applied for by the NNR on 17 June 1975, and after a public inquiry held in the parish hall at Sheringham, for which the legal costs of barrister representation for the NNR amounted to £550, the Order was transferred to the North Norfolk Railway Company on 6 April 1976.

In spite of earlier discussions and (gentlemen's) agreements, in 1982 the British Railways Property Board put up for sale by public auction Sheringham station and goods yard from the Church Street bridge eastwards to the site of the level crossing. NNR volunteers Ian Hurst and Tom Carr were sent to the auction with instructions to bid for the station and yard up to £35,000. The bidding had reached £35,000 when the representative of a property company called 'Castellan Estates' called out '40' and thereby bought the station. The new owners leased the station to the NNR, and that lease expires in 2001.

Since 1982 the railway has made great advances. It re-opened the line from Weybourne to Holt in 1989 after seven years hard labour and has introduced sophisticated semaphore signalling systems, first in the signal box at Sheringham in 1985, then at Weybourne in 1989. Since then improvements to those systems have been introduced with cleverly designed electric staff instruments for the single-line Weybourne-Holt section and between Sheringham and Weybourne. The locomotive fleet has been augmented by the big ex-GER 'B12', the only inside-cylindered 4-6-0 in the world, and also by restored diesel locomotives, one of them, the Class 37 *Mirage*, capable of 100 mph – although not on the North Norfolk Railway. It was named *Mirage* by its owner because the likelihood of it ever running again seemed at times to be as unattainable as grasping a mirage.

In 1996 101,549 people visited the NNR, of whom 91,873 travelled on the trains. In 1997 107,153 people visited, of whom 99,408 travelled. For the future the railway plans a station at Holt, in the M&GN architectural style, and a museum, the tracks to be signalled by Midland Railway wooden signals controlled from a Midland Railway signal box. At the Sheringham end of the line the feasibility of restoring the link with the national railway network is accepted in principle and is being studied in detail by the County Council and the NNR. The Ministry is even willing to allow the re-instated level crossing to be protected by traditional wooden gates, controlled from a signal box – and the original signal box for this purpose at present stands at the centre of No 2 platform at Sheringham. Everything is poised. There could be a great future for the North Norfolk Railway.

Adrian Vaughan
Barney, Norfolk

South Lynn

The 12.42 pm Peterborough-Yarmouth train arrives at South Lynn station, running past the West box, on 30 July 1956. On the left of view is the water column, filling the gap in the distant trees, beyond the River Ouse, that marks the course of the railway.

At approximately the same location on 8 April 1998 the single line of ballast in the foreground marks the line of the track between the platforms in the 'past' view. *AV Collection/AV*

The south side of South Lynn station looking north-west from the Saddlebow Road bridge on 30 July 1956. Ex-GNR 4-4-2T Class 'C12' No 67386 is possibly waiting to leave on the shuttle service to King's Lynn (GER).

In the view north-west off the Saddlebow Road bridge on 8 April 1998, the track west towards the gap in the trees, over the river, can be seen behind the central electric cable pole. The site of the former goods yard can be seen as the darker tract of ground heading towards the dual carriageway. *AV Collection/AV*

Contrasting views of the north side of South Lynn station circa 1905 and on 8 April 1998, looking south-east with the Saddlebow Road bridge in the background. *AV Collection/AV*

The east end of South Lynn station in 1958, seen from the Saddlebow Road bridge. South Lynn Junction signal box is on the left, with the connecting chord to the GER curving round behind it and the line to Melton Constable going straight on. The engine shed is on the right.

Looking east off the Saddlebow Road bridge on 8 April 1998, a huge granary now occupies the site of the old locomotive yard, and is served by a regular thunder of 38 and 44 tonne lorries. *M&GN Society (SL 59)/AV*

Gayton Road to Thursford

This is Gayton Road, 3½ miles out of South Lynn, looking east in 1955. The station's staple traffic was sand for glass-making and iron-casting. It arrived in standard gauge railway wagons along a roadside tramway that ran for three-quarters of a mile towards Gayton; the wagons were horse-drawn, but after the Great War they were hauled by petrol-engined tractors.

    The site of Gayton Road station is on the south side of the B1145 at OS 670198, and this was the view looking east on 11 October 1997. The silver birch on the right marks the end of the platform ramp. *Stations UK (4816)/AV*

Grimston Road station boasted a Midland Railway signal box, seen here looking towards South Lynn in March 1968. Grimston Road was particularly noted for the large numbers of cattle once sent away. The present-day photograph shows the scene almost exactly 30 years later, having been taken on 8 April 1998. *Brian Fisher (313/13)/AV*

This is Hillington station, also looking towards South Lynn, in 1956. The M&GN hoped that this would become a 'Royal' station to rival Wolferton on the GER Hunstanton line a few miles to the north. Photographed again late in the afternoon of 11 October 1997, the station is now part of a private dwelling. *Stations UK (5420)/AV*

Massingham was the terminus of the Lynn & Fakenham from 12 July 1879 until 16 August 1880. Set in apparently empty chalk downland, the station was three-quarters of a mile from the village of Harpley and 1½ miles from Great Massingham; the aristocratic Houghton Hall was 2 miles away. This view of the station is looking east, towards Fakenham, from the level crossing of the lane to the village. The crossing-keeper's ground frame hut is on the extreme left, its levers being released from the Midland Railway-style signal box seen at the far end of the station. The Station Master's house is on extreme right.

This is the view from the old level crossing (OS 794249) on 11 October 1997. The Station Master's house is now a doctor's surgery, and the station is fairly complete as a private dwelling; the old goods shed is still there, behind a tree, and a new building in the old style has been added on the platform of the old station. *Stations UK (5418)/ AV*

Below Massingham signal box, carefully preserved. *AV*

East Rudham station was 16¼ miles from South Lynn, and this is the office building on the up platform in about 1905. The station was once famous for its exports of grain and sugar beet. Today the building is a private dwelling, as seen on 11 October 1997. *AV Collection/AV*

Another view of East Rudham station, looking east in about 1905. Note that the signal box is too far away from the level crossing gates so they have to be worked by a porter.

The station is at OS 841264. It was impossible to replicate the old view on 11 October 1997 because the trackbed is a mass of tall brambles. *AV Collection/AV*

Below right A milepost on the down platform at East Rudham, photographed on 11 October 1997. *AV*

Opposite Raynham Park station lay half a mile from the hamlets of Tatterford and Helhoughton, but was named after the home of Lord Townsend, 1½ miles away. The signal box, which contained 21 working and three spare levers, blocks the view of the station office in this eastwards view except for a glimpse on the extreme right. A train has been set back into the Up Refuge Siding to permit a faster train to pass. The gates are superb examples of fine carpentry.

The station is at OS 867274 and is now a private dwelling. The present owners, the Hall family, treasure it and have preserved all the buildings intact; they have even added a fine old carriage on rails at the platform, as seen in this 8 April 1998 view. *AV Collection/AV*

Two views of Fakenham station in 1958 and October 1997, looking west from the barrow crossing. The site today is owned by Jewsons, the builders merchants, and a short length of the down platform has been preserved. *Stations UK (11316)/AV*

Bottom Three miles east of Fakenham was Langor Bridge level crossing and goods sidings on the A1065 at OS 961293. No photographs of the place when it was working are known, but it seems a shame to leave it out of the book, so a 'present' picture, dated 8 April 1998, is included.

In the sugar beet season it was a hive of activity, while many rail excursionists are known to have used the lavatory of the signalman's house while their train was 'waiting Line Clear' at the home signal. The level crossing lay in a valley with steep roads falling towards it on each side. In addition the eastern road approach was on a bend. The signal box was sited so that the signalman was unable to see approaching road traffic when he needed to close the gates and there were several incidents where an early-morning motor-cyclist – hurrying to get to work – narrowly escaped death as he shot through the closing gap between the level crossing gates. Eastern Counties buses, coming down the steep hill on foggy days, also had narrow escapes as the gates began to swing across their path without warning. The signalman's house, the box and the trackbed northwards are now in the hands of a restoration-minded owner. *AV*

Three and a half miles of 1 in 100 gradient from Langor Bridge brought trains to Thursford station, which would have been better named as 'Barney'. This view is looking east from the 12.30 pm Peterborough-Yarmouth train in the rain on 21 February 1959. Two more miles of near-continuous climbing will bring the train to the summit at Pigges Graves.

It was not possible to take the April 1998 view from exactly the same spot owing to a huge sheet-metal road sign, but I did use a step-ladder to simulate the height of a carriage window. The B1354 now runs between grass verges where once were platforms, while the goods shed survives behind security fencing as a Highways Depot for Norfolk CC. *AV Collection/AV*

Melton Constable

Melton Constable was the junction for Yarmouth, Norwich and Cromer, and this view, taken from the bridge over the line, shows the west side, looking south-east. One of the loco shed water tanks can be seen on the extreme right looking along the turntable track. Lord Hastings was the landowner of the district and the railway company provided him with a private waiting room and platform, seen on the extreme left. Looking almost like a continuation of the awning of the public station are the roofs and chimneys of Astley Terrace.

By 13 April 1998 the bridge over the line has been levelled and the hedges have grown tall. A step-ladder enabled me to look into the site of the old station from a spot approximately over the roof of Lord Hastings's waiting room. Thus the line of the passenger station would run out of the bottom left-hand corner of this view and extend through the caravans along the line of the fir trees in the centre. On the extreme left are three brick buildings, once part of the railway goods yard. Above the roof of the right-hand building can be seen the chimneys of Astley Terrace. In the right foreground is the gable end of a building standing on the site of the turntable. *Stations UK (6303)/AV*

An eastbound train stands at the south end of Melton's island platform in 1925. At the right edge of the view can be seen the gable end of a house, which can also be seen in the October 1997 photograph, although rather hidden behind trees. The white houses also existed in 1925 but were hidden by the locomotive. The line of the two poles and the fir trees in the 'present' picture marks the line of the tracks. *H. C. Casserley, courtesy R. M. Casserley/AV*

We are now looking north along the island platform in 1958. The goods yard buildings can be seen on the right and the loco shed water tanks on the left. As far as the October 1997 equivalent view is concerned, you'll have to take my word for the fact that there was once a busy railway junction here! *Stations UK (13113)/AV*

The locomotive and carriage & wagon works at Melton were disused when this photograph was taken, looking north, on 28 July 1937. The 'present' view shows the buildings in their present guise as a factory and lorry depot on 13 April 1998. *H. C. Casserley, courtesy R. M. Casserley/AV*

Holt and the Kelling Extension

About a mile from Melton, on the Cromer line, was Briningham Single Line Junction. The view is not repeatable today – there is no longer a tall post to climb, and at ground level a garden fence. *M&GN Society (CB 70)*

Four miles beyond Briningham the line climbed at 1 in 90 through this cutting and under the Edgefield Road bridge, number 297. A quarter of a mile beyond the bridge was Holt station. The spaniel belonged to the long-serving President of the M&GN Society, now retired, Ronald Clark, who took the picture in August 1965. The cutting has since been filled in and the Holt bypass built over it. *M&GN Society (CB 0183)/AV*

Above Holt station looking east along the down platform in 1956. The signalman has pulled off for an up train. The granary on the right was demolished with the station. The station building dated from 1926 and was constructed with concrete bricks made at Melton Constable works. *Stations UK (6305)*

Holt station building in August 1965. From careful research with a very large scale site plan and using the surviving granary as the datum point, it seems that this view, taken in April 1998, is looking through the site of the station building. *M&GN Society (CB 0189)/AV*

The down-side sidings and station at Holt, looking east, in August 1965, and the same location, now covered by the bypass, in April 1998. *M&GN Society (CB 0184)/AV*

The photographer then turned half right from the view opposite and took this view of the station. In the equivalent April 1998 picture the hedge and the oak tree on the extreme right have grown, but the right-hand of the two granaries, which has survived, can be glimpsed behind the branches. *M&GN Society (CB 0186)/AV*

At the site of the present day Holt station in January 1983, Richard ('Fozzy') Allen watches while Bernard Amies in his tractor pulls two more rails off the pile beside the Holt road; this view shows how the line was descending into a cutting to pass below a bridge over the line. Note the back of the road sign behind the rails and the leaning tree on the extreme left.

The site in April 1998 is now Holt station car park, the rear of the road sign providing the point of reference. The leaning tree is also still there, over the course of the old railway line. *Brian Fisher/AV*

Looking in the opposite direction, this was the site of the present Holt station in June 1984. A bulldozer is sheeted-up at the extreme left of the picture. Only the fir trees on the right give a clue to the location in April 1998. *Brian Fisher (970/7)/AV*

This was the station site looking south in mid-1984 and April 1998. When the cutting was filled level with its surroundings, the site was widened to the full width of the 1880 purchase to provide space for the immediate station and future developments. *Brian Fisher (970/0)/AV*

Above North Norfolk Railway progress: the line's flagship locomotive, 'B12' No 8572, arrives at Holt with a train from Sheringham. *AV*

Right Thus far and no farther: No 8572 confronts the buffers while preparing to run-round at Holt. The NNR hopes one day to break through to Fakenham. *AV*

The level crossing on Kelling Heath was installed on the orders of the Board of Trade so that people would be able to walk east to west unimpeded by the railway. Note in this February 1984 view the wind-pump to raise water for the crossing-keeper's family, and the fragment of the cast iron BEWARE OF THE TRAINS sign. The 'present' photograph was taken in April 1998. *Brian Fisher (953/30)/AV*

In February 1984 Kelling Crossing looked a lonely, lonely place made more desolate by the apparent disintegration of the track – but of course, this track is being re-laid, not taken up. The April 1998 view, again looking towards Holt, shows the track – and trains – re-instated. The cottage has also been restored by caring owners. *Brian Fisher (953/11)/AV*

Opposite A panoramic view from the east end of Kelling cutting, looking east in August 1983 and April 1998. The Distant signaļ was brought into use in March 1998. *Brian Fisher (941/10)/AV*

By May 1983 the NNR volunteers had relaid the track for a quarter of a mile on the Kelling Extension, and this small platform was built to serve the caravan site, not so far away, through the woods. This photograph was taken on the first day of passenger operation, 28 August 1983.

When the Kelling Extension was opened to Holt, Kelling Camp Halt was demolished and a new, larger platform was built a quarter of a mile further up the hill. The long-serving, hard-working railbus was laid up for repairs in April 1998, its place being taken by Tim Moore's diesel multiple unit (DMU), on contract with the North Norfolk Railway. *Brian Fisher (941/2)/AV*

Weybourne

Looking up the 1 in 80 incline of Kelling bank towards Holt, 40 miles from South Lynn, a train from Norwich and Melton Constable approaches Weybourne on 23 October 1963. Note that the facing points have been dismantled. By August 1965 all the track has gone. *Peter Waylett/Brian Fisher (R64/6)*

This February 1983 photograph shows relaying of the Kelling Extension in progress at Springbeck bridge, looking towards Holt, and demonstrates how relatively few people were actually involved, day to day, on this heavy project. As with all restored railways a great deal was achieved by a small group of highly motivated people for the benefit of tens of thousands. The finished trackwork in October 1997 looks as if it had never been dismantled.
Brian Fisher (909/31)/AV

46

The first view of Weybourne station, from the lane overbridge, is looking towards Sheringham in 1956. The garden is neatly tended but loneliness seems to be the strongest impression. Note the lack of a footbridge.

By 23 October 1963, the date of the second picture, all signals and the signal box have been removed.

By March 1968 the waiting shelter has also been removed. The replacement NNR signal box was transferred by road lorry from Holt in 1967; the white rectangle of clean paint below the gable end window is where the short 'HOLT' nameboard was fixed. It was eventually brought into service in the summer of 1990.

The final photograph shows the restored station in October 1997. The waiting shelter was rebuilt new by John Lavercombe and brought into use in the spring of 1987, while the footbridge, rescued from Stowmarket, was brought into use in summer 1990. *Stations UK (6308)/Peter Waylett/Brian Fisher (312/8)/AV*

The general view of the station, looking towards Holt, dates from 1924. By July 1971, the date of the second photograph, children are playing on the derelict track.

The third view was taken in January 1983, towards the end of a year-long refurbishment. The station had been re-roofed, and heavy repairs to the interior and main beams had also been carried out during 1982.

Finally we see the station building in April 1998. Because of rot found in the supporting beams in 1982, these were replaced and the canopy was given supporting columns – made from old superheater flues from the 'B12'.
Stations UK (3017)/M&GN Society (CB 0196)/Brian Fisher (906/36)/AV

49

Contrasting views of Weybourne: the first was taken from the down platform, looking towards Holt, in June 1966, while the second, taken in April 1998, is the definitive view from the new footbridge. The place looks in better condition than for 50 years. *Brian Fisher (R64)/AV*

The view east from the footbridge, and (*below*) the present-day track and signalling layout at Weybourne. *AV*

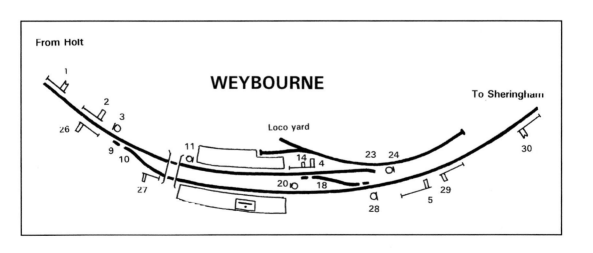

The cattle or horse-loading dock at Weybourne in 1970. Today the 'dock' is usually full with its complement of valuable rolling-stock, but in April 1998 the vehicles were removed by obliging NNR volunteers. *M&GN Society (CB 122)/AV*

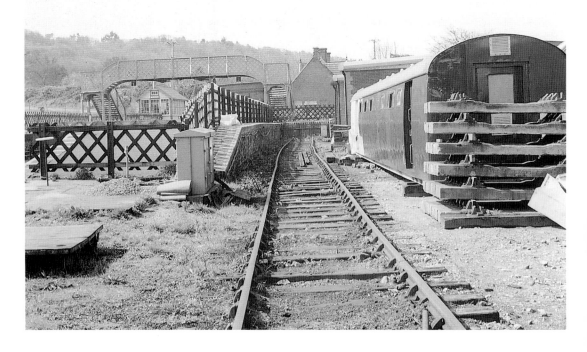

The first photograph shows track relaying at the Sheringham end of the down platform, looking towards Sheringham in June 1966, while the second is the scene as viewed from the up platform circa 1974.

In the third picture we see the 1966 view replicated in April 1998 after many years of labour, and what a remarkable transformation! No 4 signal is seen cleared to permit a movement over the power-operated facing points to the Down Main line. The small signal arm is No 14 and routes to the sidings. These controls were installed when the signal box was commissioned during 1990. The neat hut houses a 'ground frame', electrically unlocked when the Weybourne signal box is switched out of circuit, from which the locomotive men can operate the power points. This is an installation dating from 1986 replacing the original two-lever ground frame working facing points and bolts. *Brian Fisher (R64/10)/M&GN Society (CB 119)/ AV*

The Holt end of Weybourne station looking towards Sheringham in July 1971 and October 1997; the contrast strongly emphasises the huge progress made by the North Norfolk Railway in the intervening years. Note in the 'present' view the Train Staff setting-down column – otherwise known as the 'cow's horn' – by the pier of the bridge. *M&GN Society (CB 0201)/AV*

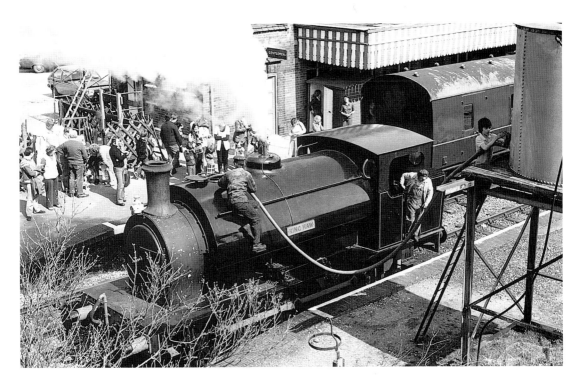

Ring Haw, from Nassington Quarry, Peterborough, the 'Black Five' of the North Norfolk Railway, stands at the Holt end of Weybourne station taking water in the summer of 1979. The water tank was raised and the trestle built by a pair of local farmers.

The splendidly correct water column was brought into use in March 1981. For this April 1998 photograph the train crew obligingly positioned their locomotive but, unfortunately for a strict copy of the 'past' view, did not have time to take water. *Brian Fisher (595/25)/AV*

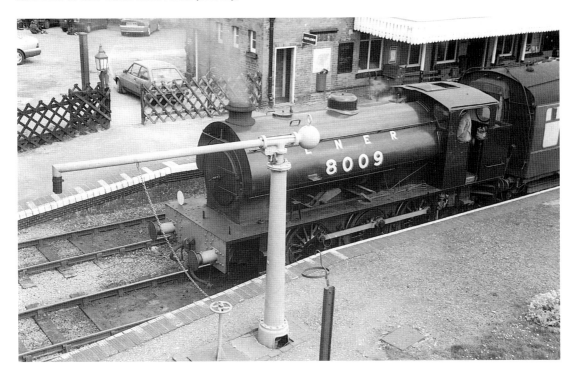

Weybourne station and yard from the east, in March 1978 and January 1997. The yard has been enlarged and the speed limit over the facing points raised by 50 per cent. *Brian Fisher/AV*

The west end of Weybourne yard in June 1984 and April 1998. The spot from which the 'past' view was taken has been covered by a grounded coach body, so I stood on the roof of the coach to replicate the view. Much labour has been expended, not only by volunteers but also by men sent in by the Manpower Services Commission, supervised by NNR experts. In 1976 the NNR received £14,000-worth of labour from the government scheme.
Brian Fisher (970/82)/AV

In the summer of 1976 the engine shed at Weybourne is under construction. The steelwork was dismantled by volunteers from the 1942 LNER loco shed at Norwich City; the original M&GN shed having been destroyed in the Norwich blitz.

When viewed from the same angle as in the previous shot in April 1998 the engine shed is obscured by the workshop brought into use in 1991. *Brian Fisher (501/25)/AV*

Above The well-lit workshop is also well equipped and is a far cry from the stupendously spartan conditions under which volunteers once worked on locomotives and other machinery. *AV*

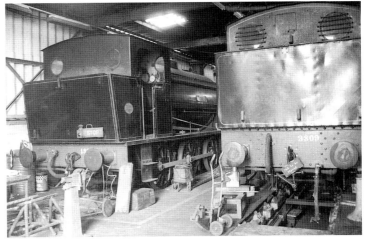

Right The engine shed is also well-equipped and practical. The engines are still filthy, oily, sweaty things to work on, especially when a driving wheel spring or axle-box needs to be removed, working from within the confines of the pit – but at least the worker is in the dry and well lit – he creates his own heat! *AV*

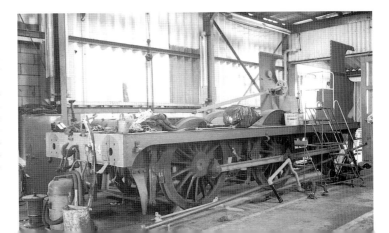

Right This is the Midland & Great Northern Society's famous ex-Great Eastern Railway 'J15' locomotive stripped to the frames and well on the way to full restoration. At the time of the photograph, one of its drivers, Barry Sutton-Jones, was between the frames wielding a paint brush loaded with pink primer paint. Photos taken in April 1998. *AV*

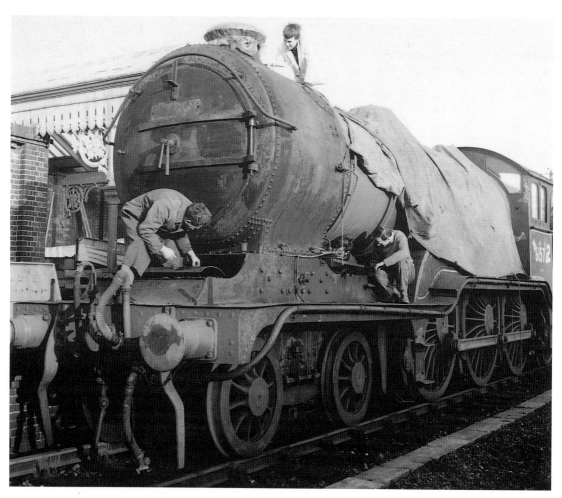

This ex-Great Eastern '1500' Class 4-6-0, reboilered under the LNER to become Class 'B12', is the sole surviving inside-cylindered 10-wheeled engine in the world. It is seen in the first photograph (*opposite above*) at Sheringham in January 1969, not long after its delivery from British Railways.

The restoration of the 'B12' has been, perhaps, the greatest struggle in the history of the North Norfolk Railway. The second view shows it standing on the concrete pad specially constructed for it at Weybourne in May 1985, still awaiting major repairs.

The third picture (*left*) is of the locomotive's firebox end awaiting restoration in June 1984, followed by a photograph of the footplate of the finished locomotive with a fire in her belly in April 1998 (*above*).

After being sent to East Germany for boiler restoration, the engine is now very much the flagship of the North Norfolk Railway, and the 'apple of the railway's eye' in her Apple Green livery. The final photograph shows her at Sheringham in April 1998.
Brian Fisher (R84/7)/AV/Brian Fisher (970/85)/AV (2)

Bridge 303 over the A149, between Weybourne and Sheringham, was nearly life-expired when purchased by the North Norfolk Railway in 1971, the year in which this photograph was taken.

A set of second-hand girders from Shippea Hill, near Ely, was purchased from British Rail early in 1983 and brought by rail and road to Sheringham. There they were sand-blasted to clean them thoroughly, then shortened to fit the site, before being taken by road to the site. The A149 was closed and they were raised into position by a somewhat stressed road crane. *M&GN Society (CB 0200)/AV*

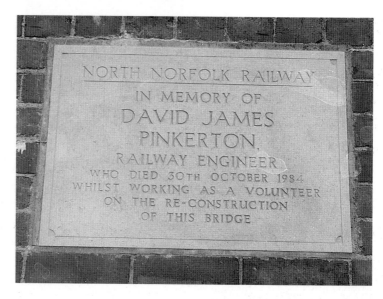

The work was directed by David Pinkerton, a British Rail bridge engineer, who most sadly and tragically lost his life while working on the bridge. *AV*

Sheringham

The Peckett and the 'Quad-art' coaches form a train from Weybourne to Sheringham at Sweet Briar Lane or Golf Links Crossing during the Easter weekend of 1971. The legs and flag of the hand-signalman, protecting road and rail traffic at the crossing, can just be glimpsed in the space below the right-hand buffer of the engine and the gate post.

On 3 May 1998, after two more systems for protecting road/rail traffic, this is the final development: flashing lights in both directions, the warnings activated or cancelled by rail-mounted treadles, one of which can be seen in the foreground. *Brian Fisher (R91)/AV*

Looking east across Sheringham station from Church Street bridge in 1952 we see a busy scene, with a train for Cromer, with through carriages from London via North Walsham, in Platform 3, and the shunting of coal trucks blocking the platform road. The signal was worked from East box and 'slotted' by West box.

The second photograph was taken in 1964 after the train service had been terminated westwards beyond Sheringham and the old West box abolished. A garden is developing on the left-hand side of the picture.

One of the earliest restorations on the North Norfolk Railway was to re-site and re-paint the old East box, bringing it from the far road to the centre of the platform. The third picture shows the view in November 1975.

Finally we see the scene in October 1997 – as good as new. *Stations UK (RR 2A56 & UK 26221)/Brian Fisher (401/23)/AV*

Looking now from the north end of the Church Street bridge (*opposite above*), we can see that six-wheeled carriages were still in use as late as 1956, and that electric lighting is being installed on the platforms.

From 1967 until early 1982 Sheringham station had to be used as a workshop, which meant that a lot of tidying-up had to be done on Fridays ready for the arrival of the weekend tourists. This was the scene in 1977 (*opposite below*), with the NNR's locomotive fleet on show – not all of it operational.

The third photograph shows the well-ordered scene in April 1998. *Stations UK (R8328)/Brian Fisher/AV*

(18)—V 20—10,000—1-11.   [W. & S. Ltd.]
MIDLAND & GREAT NORTHERN RAILWAYS JOINT COMMITTEE.

From_____
TO

SHERINGHAM

The first of these three views of Sheringham station from the south end of the Church Road bridge was taken in 1957. By January 1975, the date of the second photograph, the tracks into Platform 3 and yard had been lifted, while the third view shows the grand improvement in **April 1998.** *M&GN Society (CB 6)/ Brian Fisher/AV*

In March 1967 the railway still crossed the main road, although by then BR trains terminated at a platform to the east of the road. A DMU is standing there and preservationists are de-training, while others are pouring on to the track from the old station platform. They are on a rail tour and will go by bus to Weybourne.

The 'present' photograph is from approximately the same camera position in October 1997. *Brian Fisher (305/11)/AV*

In 1964 this was the view westwards from where the main road into the town crossed the railway on the level, while in the October 1997 equivalent the NNR station can be seen beyond the bushes in the background. *Stations UK 26222/AV*

Looking south over the level crossing in April 1969, and the same view in April 1998; the present-day arrangement looks permanent enough, but there is a possibility that the railway will return once more across the road. *M&GN Society (CB 219)/AV*

Above The level crossing was abolished in 1969 but was re-instated for a few hours on 15/16 March 1975 in order to bring rolling-stock on to the NNR. There were two weeks of intensive planning, but the actual process of laying the rails across the road was a matter of laborious muscle-power. *Brian Fisher (412/2)*

Below The last steam engine – for the time being – to cross the main road at Sheringham was *Colwyn*, hauling a 1943-built ex-Southern Railway 12-ton capacity hand-winched crane on 16 March 1975. *Colwyn* was built by Kitson & Co in 1933 and was used in the ironstone quarries of Stewarts & Lloyds. It was purchased by NNR Chairman Bernard Amies in 1968. *Brian Fisher (412/8)*

The 0-4-0 80 hp Fowler diesel-mechanical shunter, known on the NNR as 'Doctor Harry', was a sorry mess when purchased by the Fenland Group of the NNR, but it returned to useful service on 16 February 1974 and here is hauling the works train off the temporary level crossing on 16 March 1975.

In April 1998 the North Norfolk Railway, temporarily truncated, lies waiting patiently, pointing at the gap in the houses only 150 yards away and its natural route into Cromer. Maybe it won't be long before the rust comes off those rails. . . *Brian Fisher (412/35)/AV*

At the west end of Sheringham station in January 1969 the volunteers, under John Keutgen, are fitting a facing point bolt to a facing point; then hand-lever-operated, it will be worked from a remote ground frame (pictured on page 82) when the project is complete. They have erected a starting signal post in the middle of the space that they will require for the Platform 2 line.

In April 1977 the points are worked from the remote ground frame, the signal post has been dug up to make way for the Platform 2 track, and a locomotive inspection pit has been dug, the latter during May 1976.

The scene in April 1998. The fine lattice-mast signals were brought into use in 1985. The locomotive inspection pit, dug out in 1970, was filled in *circa* 1996. *Brian Fisher (84/10 & 498/13)/AV*

The 'past' photograph takes us back again to 1969; the points, their bolt and the signals have now been connected to the remote ground frame, although the old hand-lever is still in place.

After years of work, full conventional signalling, worked from a proper signal box, was brought into use during the first half of 1985. This is the same location in April 1998. *M&GN Society (CB 46)/AV*

Looking south in February 1978 as the station grows, Platform tracks 2 and 3 are both now laid, and the Gresley 'Quad-arts' (Set 74) are under Church Street bridge.

In April 1998 the railbus was out of action and had to be towed into position by a Class 08 shunter, in the midst of a busy station operating day, to enable the equivalent photograph to be taken. *Brian Fisher/AV*

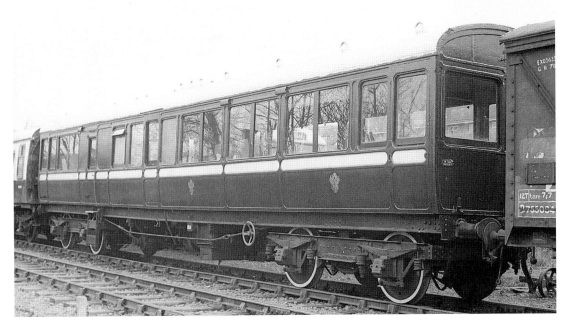

The Lancashire & Yorkshire Railway Directors' official conveyance (and that of the London & North Western Railway) was saved from destruction by fire at the BR concentration camp for aristocratic carriages at Wymondham-Ashwelthorpe by the vigilance of an NNR volunteer, John Rumens. They both arrived at Sheringham on 26 May 1969 in good condition.

Sadly there was neither the time, the money nor the labour to restore everything, so the poor old saloon is still living in hope of resurrection. It is seen here in April 1998. *Brian Fisher/AV*

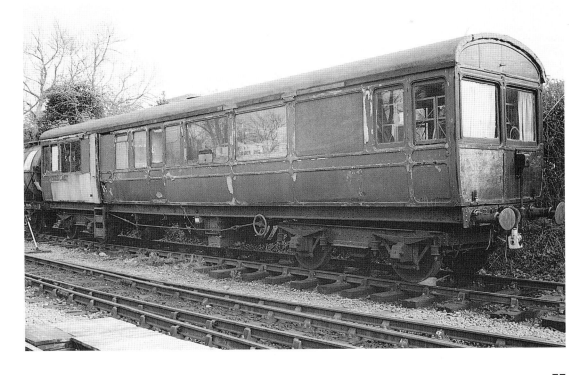

The Gresley-era buffet car was preserved in 1978 and over the years was stripped down and the body removed from the bogies for a complete refit, new wooden parts being made where necessary. Seen in the first photograph under the bridge at Sheringham early in 1981, the entire interior, complete with a new kitchen, had to be rebuilt. Years of hard work received their reward when the coach was returned to service in full working order in 1988, and is seen in all its glory at Sheringham in April 1998. *Brian Fisher (2)/AV (2)*

The mainstay of NNR train services in the beginning was *Colwyn*, seen here, and the Peckett, hauling either the 'Quad-art' articulated set or the suburban coaches. Some very magnificent trains were also possible, since the railway had two 'Brighton Belle' Pullman coaches and the Directors' saloons. The first photograph was taken in April 1975.

Two years later *Colwyn* and the 'Quad-arts' leave Sheringham on 11 April 1977. The manner in which the first and second coach share a common bogie can be seen. Immediately ahead of the engine is the signal for incoming trains, and to the right of that is the 1969 ground frame, the levers at the level of the top-most signal arm, the space below the levers boarded in. The North Norfolk Railway was built up, layer by layer, painfully, as the money and the time became available – but the volunteers never gave up.

In April 1998 the 'Quad-arts' were standing at Weybourne awaiting a thorough restoration.
Brian Fisher (413/3 & 498/17)/AV

Above Most work in the first 20 years was done in situations completely open to the weather or in this space on Sheringham platform, under the glass awning and known sarcastically as 'Melton Works'. Carpenter Neil Stevens is at work on the platform in the freezing weather of February 1978. This area is now covered by the Refreshment Room (see page 88). *Brian Fisher (548/1)*

Right Meanwhile, across two tracks, someone else is suffering from a freezing backside, possibly Nick Johnson, since welding is involved. *Brian Fisher (548/0)*

Above The Sheringham ground frame under construction in May 1969. *Brian Fisher (323/20)*

Below In April 1979 *Ring Haw* is about to pass the vacant site of the old Sheringham West signal box, on the extreme left of the photograph, on which will be placed the new box. *Brian Fisher (595/30)*

The new signal box was brought from Wensum Junction, Norwich, on 4 August 1982 and dropped over the fence on to a waiting 'Lowmac' wagon. *Brian Fisher (887/21 & 887/31)*

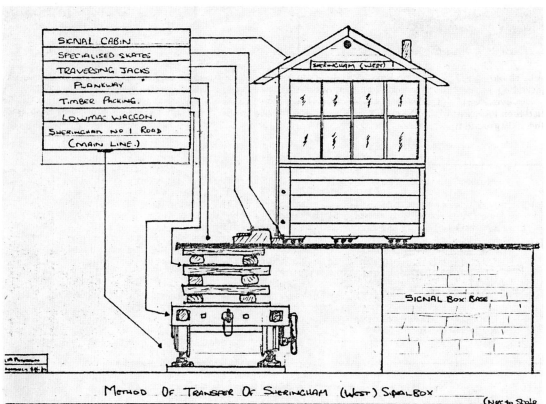

SIGNAL CABIN
SPECIALISED SKATES
TRAVERSING JACKS
PLANKWAY
TIMBER PACKING.
LOWMAC WAGGON.
SHERINGHAM NO 1 ROAD
(MAIN LINE.)

SHERINGHAM (WEST)

SIGNAL BOX BASE.

METHOD OF TRANSFER OF SHERINGHAM (WEST) SIGNALBOX

(NOT TO SCALE)

A brick base was built by Fred Poynter and a group from the Youth Opportunities Programme, and the box was jacked up, supported on sleepers and, as seen here, rolled across to its final position on 13 January 1983.

However, the complications had only just begun, because the signal box mechanical and electrical machinery had then to be installed. The signal seen in front of the box in this March 1983 photograph was still worked by the 1969 ground frame. *Eastern Daily Press/Brian Fisher*

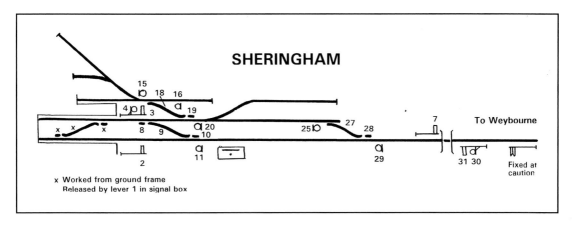

The present-day track and signalling layout at Sheringham.

Opposite and above The heavy ironwork of the lever frame takes up position in April 1983. New interlocking had to be cut from steel plate and electric circuits designed, by John Keutgen, and wired to the instruments by him and Philip Handford-Rice. A continuous commitment over years was required to see the job through.

Fred Poynter, seen in the second photograph from January 1984, played a major role in fitting the frame and now, after a year, has the lighter duty of painting the levers.

Again, virtue brings its own reward, and years of effort produced this splendid signal box, photographed in April 1996. The lever frame was reclaimed from a redundant ex-GER signal box at Leyton in East London, while the splendid 'tablet' instrument on the extreme right came from Cromer M&GN. *Brian Fisher (912/20 & 952/53)/AV*

Below Sheringham West box looks as if it has always been there, as *Ring Haw* approaches with a Sunday Pullman Diner in September 1994. *AV*

This space on Sheringham station platform was originally where the town's parcels and passengers' trunks and boxes where stacked awaiting delivery or the train. The double doors on the left were wide to allow for large loads to pass through. The area was subsequently used as a workshop by the NNR (see page 81), but here in January 1984 Fred Poynter (right) and others are clearing up prior to the space being converted into a Refreshment Room and kitchen.

The second photograph shows the site as seen from a rail wagon, while upon completion Fred Poynter's remarkably authentic woodwork fooled me and doubtless many others into assuming that the Refreshment Room had been built by the M&GN. *Eastern Daily Press/Brian Fisher (952/57)/AV*

The splendid glass-roofed refreshment room, light and bright, was created with considerable imagination out of a rather dark hole. The site of the original double doors, seen opposite, is the protruding section of the left-hand wall on which are mounted the signal arms. *AV*

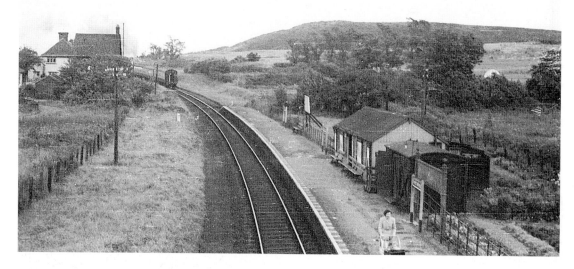

Sheringham to Cromer

The 'past' picture shows West Runton Halt looking towards Cromer in about 1949. Today an informal partnership between the present franchisee of the Cromer-Sheringham line, Anglia Trains, and Mrs Bullock, who wants to encourage people to go by train, has created a modern halt with a traditional yet 'up-to-the-minute' look. The gardens are the result of Mrs Bullock's efforts and the glass waiting shelter is courtesy of Anglia Trains, while the rebuilt M&GN nameboard is the work of local M&GN enthusiast Nigel Digby. All trains stop here and provide the village with a connecting service to London and the Midlands. *Stations UK (R8327)/AV*

Bridge 315 was near Cromer Gas Works, about a quarter of a mile short of Cromer M&GN station. In 1906 the M&GN Joint Committee and the Great Eastern co-operated in making a connection between the two railways at Cromer, creating the necessity for doubling the track. The earthworks appear to have been made wide enough for this in 1887. The cutting side was, however, cut back and drains laid. The works train drawn by the locomotive *Alpha* is on a temporary trestle bridge.

At bridge 315 in April 1998 what appears to be double track is in fact two single tracks: the nearest is the Norwich-Cromer line, the other the Cromer-Sheringham. *AV Collection/AV*

This is Cromer (Beach) station seen from the end of the loading dock behind the signal box (left) in 1960. In April 1998 the loading dock was filled with large trees, so this 'present' view was taken from the top of the signal box steps. *M&GN Society (CB 0390)/AV*

Cromer (Beach) signal box was built of M&GN concrete blocks made at Melton Constable. These two views are looking towards Sheringham in February 1959 and April 1998. *M&GN Society (CB 0252)/AV*

Cromer (Beach) station looking outwards from the buffers in 1954, and as near as possible the same view in October 1997. *Stations UK (R8321)/AV*

The station offices at Cromer were leased to Travis & Arnold, the builders merchants, from about 1965 and were kept in good order by them, but when they vacated the premises the building fell into a bad state. It was sold, along with the old station yard, to Sainsburys and in April 1998 was in the process of restoration. Perhaps it will be completed in time to welcome the North Norfolk Railway into the station! *M&GN Society (CB 0140)/AV*

INDEX